THINGS SEEN

WINNER OF FRENCH VOICES AWARD

www.frenchbooknews.com

THINGS
SEEN

Annie Ernaux

Translated by Jonathan Kaplansky
Foreword by Brian Evenson

University of Nebraska Press
Lincoln and London

Foreword and translation
© 2010 by the Board of Regents
of the University of Nebraska
Originally published in French
as *La vie extérieure* © Éditions
Gallimard, Paris, 2000.

French Voices Logo designed
by Serge Bloch.

Cet ouvrage, publié dans le
cadre d'un programme d'aide
à la publication, bénéficie du
soutien financier du ministère
des Affaires étrangères, du
Service culturel de l'ambassade
de France aux États-Unis, ainsi
que de l'appui de FACE (French
American Cultural Exchange).

This work, published as
part of a program providing
publication assistance, received
financial support from the
French Ministry of Foreign
Affairs, the Cultural Services
of the French Embassy in the
United States and FACE (French
American Cultural Exchange).

Library of Congress Cataloging-
in-Publication Data

Ernaux, Annie, 1940–
[Vie extérieure. English]
Things seen / Annie Ernaux;
translated by Jonathan Kaplansky;
foreword by Brian Evenson.
p. cm.
ISBN 978-0-8032-1077-6 (cloth:
alk. paper) — ISBN 978-0-8032-
2815-3 (pbk.: alk. paper)
1. Ernaux, Annie, 1940—Diaries.
2. Authors, French—20th
century—Diaries. I. Kaplansky,
Jonathan, 1960– II. Title.
PQ2665.R67Z47813 2010
848'91403—dc22
[B]
2009028606

Set in Galliard by Kim Essman.
Designed by Nathan Putens.

Foreword

Brian Evenson

Annie Ernaux is best known for having few compunctions about mining her own life — and the lives of those close to her — to create work with one foot seemingly in fiction and the other in memoir. In unembellished but precise prose she examines this personal territory with care, detachment, and candor. Her first novel, *Cleaned Out* (1974), tells the story of a young woman who has just had an abortion and who begins painfully to reexamine her life — a subject Ernaux returns to (in a less fictionalized form) in *Happening* (2000). In *A Man's Place* (1984) and a *Woman's Story* (1987) she explores the lives of the conservative parents she has distanced herself from. *I Remain in Darkness* (1997) explores her mother's descent into dementia. *Simple Passion* (1991) chronicles a woman's love affair with a man only identified as "A." A later book, *Se Perdre* [To Lose Oneself] (2001), takes the same subject up again in journal form, though A. has been replaced by "S." In other books Ernaux explores childhood memories, the experience of becoming a woman and having children, and her struggle against breast cancer.

The intimacy of her subject matter, the unwavering objectivity with which she presents it, and the way she blurs the line between the fictional and the real are what give Ernaux's work its strength. It is quietly detached and quite unflinchingly and candidly honest. Her prose makes little attempt to provide an alibi or justification either for her characters or for herself. Instead, she attempts to capture as nakedly as possible what it means to be a woman from a certain background who has made certain choices. She is interested in doing this not in the abstract but in particular, both in how choices large and small can form one person and how to convey all the minutiae of that person's life, all the objects and disjecta that envelop it, in a way that will resonate for others.

Things Seen was published in France in 2000 as *La vie extériure*, a title that might be translated as "Exterior Life" or "The Life Outside." It is a loose collection of jottings that Ernaux, or her narrator (the "I" is never named and a deliberate ambiguity remains — it is either Ernaux or a woman very much like her), makes about the world around her. The narrator offers us fleeting moments of her impressions and preoccupations, things experienced on the train or in the supermarket, things heard on the radio, things seen on TV. Presented as a journal, on one level the book seems deeply personal. However, most of the details Ernaux records are highly impersonal; as the French title suggests, they are scenes from exterior life, things that might happen to anyone, things that come by chance, encountered and quickly forgotten: a tramp trying to sell newspapers; the way someone looks on a subway platform; minor events while in line at a store; a fire in a subway tunnel; images of war on television.

In *Se Perdre*, as she recounts the details of her love affair, Ernaux admits, "Le monde extérieur est presque totalement absent de ces pages" (The outside world is nearly completely absent from these pages). *Things Seen*, however, presents just the opposite: the outside world is nearly all there is. At the same time, everything about this outside world is selected by and processed through one person, one writer. Despite her reticence, an image of her begins to form according to what she notices, and the original but eccentric way in which she renders the world. (Who else, for instance, would compare a man's amputated leg stumps to "the tips of two huge penises"?) By refusing to give readers the character and plot markers they usually hold onto, *Things Seen* becomes profoundly bound up in perception and develops a subtle contact with one person's embodied vision of the transient world.

Like many of Ernaux's books, *Things Seen* returns to a territory she has already touched upon — in this case, to the earlier *Journal du dehors* [Journal of the Outside], published in 1993 and translated into English as *Exteriors*. *Exteriors* explores Ernaux's interactions with the exterior world of life in a "new town" located forty kilometers outside Paris, between 1985 and 1992. It shows glimpses of encounters on the metro, on the train, in stores, etc., as she explores a life she feels both alienated from and drawn to. Unlike *Things Seen*, in which every entry is dated, *Exteriors* simply organizes entries by year. Lengths vary dramatically, ranging from nearly a third of the total book for 1986, to a mere two pages for 1990. The seven total chapters of *Things Seen* are a little more regular, with the shortest accounting for a fourteenth of the book and the longest (the first chapter) one quarter of the whole. Generally speaking, in the earlier *Exteriors* there is a higher level of uncertainty and discomfort both in terms of the life described and formally, as well as some commentary on the form itself. Indeed, two-thirds of the way through the book the narrator describes herself as "traversée par les gens, leur existence, comme une putain" (passed through by people, by their existence, like a whore). Two thirds of the way through *Things Seen*, that book's narrator feels quite differently: "For the first time I have taken possession of space that I have been traveling through for twenty years."

Ernaux (or her doppleganger) is not the focus of *Things Seen*, but we nonetheless see little glimpses of the author — intimations of her history, her life. A couple hugging and kissing remind her of "F.", whom she hugged and kissed at the same spot, though we learn nothing more about F. than this. She walks down a street and remembers she walked down it on another occasion to go see "Doctor M.", though she does not say why she was seeing the doctor. She mentions a "we" going to a political demonstration, but who the other part of that "we" is she never says. "They" visit her, "they" watch *X-Files* and play video games, and she does two loads of "his" laundry. When she finally does identify them, she does so in an impersonal way, as if they are not connected to her at all: "nothing personal: the Sunday of a single woman whose son comes to see her with his girlfriend, in the Paris area."

There are also a few pseudo-personal moments: a film is described in such a way that at first the reader doesn't know it's a film (as opposed to something being directly experienced). Indeed, the narrator often seems as affected by what she experiences through film or television as she does by the real events of her life. One of the major tensions of the book is the friction between news from afar and the substance of the day-to-day life around us. We can feel concerned about Princess Diana's death because "it requires nothing from us except tears for the injustice of destiny. It consoles." It doesn't importune us in the same way the homeless woman at the bottom of the metro stairs does. Nor, on the other hand, does it make us ashamed of doing nothing as a war broadcast might.

"From the baby carriage to the grave, life unfolds more and more between the shopping center and the television set," Ernaux's narrator suggests. This continuum is, the narrator admits, "no more strange or absurd" than the way life unfolded in the past, "in fields or cafés, or at evening gatherings." Yet living in such a continuum creates an anxiety: the fear of being lost in the rush and sweep of the crowd, of being swallowed up "by the wave of anonymous people that I encounter and of which, for the others, I am a part."

The philosophical paradox that for yourself you are an individual, but for another in the exterior world you are part of the anonymous largely undifferentiated crowd is punctuated by the anonymity of the narrator herself, by her own reticence to reveal personal details. She is an individual who deliberately isn't fleshed out to be a character, yet she still feels real. She is someone who hesitates in the interval between the particular and the anonymous.

Focused on the transient nature of life and our perception of it, *Exteriors* and *Things Seen* both shiver on the edge of significance. They read like journals or diaries but are slightly more shaped, more focused, without seeming any less natural. They are intimate in the sense that they feel as if they were not written to be read by an outsider, but distant in that they reveal very little to us directly about the person writing them. Instead, they are, as she suggests in her introduction to *Exteriors*, "a series of snapshots reflecting the daily life of a community." They hold together just enough, while at the same time resisting a transformation into "the literary." The reason for this resistance is perhaps suggested by words that come late in *Thing Seen*, from a phrase to which the book owes its title: "Things seen in the outside world require everything; most works of art, nothing."

The hesitation, the attempt to stay in the interval between a work of art and the actual world, puts demands on the reader that are different from what is normally expected from either a journal or a literary work. *Things Seen* at once asks everything of us, and nothing. It is a deceptively simple book, and a profoundly disarming one.

THINGS SEEN

1993

April 3

In the RER, at Cergy-Préfecture, three girls board, and a boy with jeans torn at the knee and a pendant hanging from a chain.

One girl to another: "You smell good."

"It's Minidou."

The boy: "Renaud is playing in *Germinal*."

A girl: "So what, it's just a movie."

The boy justifies himself: "I love Renaud and Zola, so . . . " They are going to Virgin Records.

It is the Saturday RER, with groups of young people and families going to Paris. An atmosphere of plans and desires can be read on the faces, in the bodies, eager to sit down and stand up. La Défense is deserted. People get off at l'Étoile, at Auber, at Les Halles, where music is already there to greet them.

Returning from Paris: evening. A couple with two children. The little boy falls asleep as soon as he sits down, mouth tightly closed, looking old. The little girl, five or six, blond with glasses, is fidgeting back and forth. She is wearing shiny pantyhose, Chantal Thomass style, a bit perverse. The father looks at his daughter's legs and repeats, "pull down your skirt, what's the point of having one." The mother, dressed without any interest in her appearance, does not seem to hear.

April 8

Condominium meeting. People talk about staircases, basements, etc. Every issue tackled becomes an opportunity for people to show their knowledge, "we need to install meters at such and such a place," to tell an anecdote "in the building where I lived before," a story "the other day, the tenant on the fifth floor." Stories are a need to exist.

Ever since universities have opened in Cergy, students can be seen in the evening at Auchan doing their shopping. Recognizable at the cash by a somewhat ironic distance, spontaneously banding together, not needing to say hello to one another, like people accustomed to seeing each other all day long in class or in the university cafeteria. These are people brought together by shared activities (the same rooms, schedules, interests), fleeting and intense.

April 13

In the RER to Cergy an Asian woman is knitting, a pattern spread out over her knees. It appears very complicated, three balls of wool in various colors on the paper of the pattern and whose strands she takes in turn. I am reading *Le Monde*, an article on what is happening in Bosnia. In view of this war my activity is not much more useful than hers. Eighteen years ago, in the same way, I must have read an article about the boat people: perhaps she was one. Just before Conflans, she takes out a key ring that works as scissors, cuts the strands, puts away the balls of yarn and the work in her bag, stands up to leave.

April 17

Flight from Marseilles to Paris. The woman next to the window wears a mauve pantsuit, a lighter colored mauve blouse, with a small black and gold purse, and matching shoes. She is not reading. She begins to file her nails carefully. She looks at herself in a mirror. Later, she opens and closes her purse, searching for something, or not. When the flight attendant goes by with the refreshment cart, she asks for champagne, pays for it, drinks slowly, looking in front of her. This is a woman going to join a man, treating herself to champagne to make the joy of expectation perfect. Celebrating expectation itself.

Before landing, she looks at herself in the mirror again, touches up her makeup. It is as if I were her.

That evening, at Les Halles, a black with a kind of cymbals, another is beating a drum, a third singing. A drunken white dances near them with a doll stuck in the belt of his pants. Travelers crowd around. I remember my dream, at sixteen, to go live in Harlem, because of the jazz.

May 11

Near Bonne-Nouvelle station, a fat guy of about thirty calls out to me. I ask him what he wants. He shows me a cup: "To eat!" I remark to him, laughing, that he appears to be in good health. He takes out a brochure from his pocket for a weight loss clinic; he was supposed to go there, but is not covered by Social Security. We talk, he about his situation, me about how hard it is to respond to all requests. He is holding a classified ad newspaper and a small sign. Carefully he spreads out the newspaper on one of the stairs leading down to the subway and sits down, setting down the sign and the cup. He says, "I swear to you I don't drink" and approaching me, "besides, if I drank, you'd smell the wine, the alcohol." And also, "there's no more dignity anywhere."

May 18

At the Yves Saint Laurent hosiery counter at Le Printemps on Boulevard Haussmann no saleswoman is present. At the other end of the counter, a woman is rummaging through packages of pantyhose. Quickly she slips one of them into her purse and walks toward the perfume counter. All of a sudden I understand that she has just stolen a pair of pantyhose. Since I was not paying particular attention to her, something out of place in the expected sequence of her movements — stuffing the object into her purse instead of holding it in her hand while heading toward the cash — must have alerted me unconsciously.

I imagine this woman's heady feeling.

May 20

Bars on the window of the "Jean-Claude Monderer" shoe store at Trois-Fontaines, and a sign: "Closing Sale: Everything Must Go." A store that was called "Espace 2 M" when I arrived in the new town. I try to remember all the pairs of shoes I bought here.

Each disappearance of a store in the shopping center signifies the death of a part of oneself, where longing is strongest.

May 21

A woman wearing no makeup sits across from her preteen son, in the RER to Denfert. She is reading a women's magazine. He is shifting his legs, hiding his head behind his school bag: all signs indicate that he doesn't know what to do with his body. He talks, asks his mother questions. She doesn't answer. The article she is reading is entitled "Age is No Longer an Obstacle to Love."

May 22

A highly-rated Strasbourg "Weinstube," Chez Yvonne, tables are close together, creating artificial friendliness. A couple, in their fifties. They take out the GaultMillau and order the "presskopf" recommended in the guide. Waiting for the dish, they say that they are from the Paris area, are taking the wine route over the long Ascension Day weekend. They smile. Once served, they only speak to comment upon what they are eating. Perhaps this is how they move from one plan to the next, guided noon and night by the GaultMillau, which for them has replaced the manual of *Lovemaking Techniques*, if they ever read it.

May 28

While channel-hopping as usual before turning off the TV, I saw the smooth and beautiful face of a very young girl appear on screen. She was saying "my father raped me when I was twelve." It was impossible to leave this face. She calmly continued her story — the mother would fall asleep with sleeping pills every day, the father would sneak into the child's bedroom — helped along by the discreet questions of the host, a middle-aged, gray-haired man, looking like a good father, playing the role of confidant. Then the mother arrived, with her tortured face, on the verge of tears, then the grandmother, a strong woman defending her son the rapist, currently in prison and who "is crying like a baby."

In the following act the village appears; its inhabitants, present on the set, accuse the girl of having played a role, of even provoking her father. The girl, head held high, resembles an ancient heroine facing a furious chorus.

Third act. Psychiatrists and a lawyer enter the scene, explain and resolve the conflict. 1) the father raped his daughter because he himself was raped as a child by a family member; 2) the little girl, in his power, had no choice but to accept the rape; 3) the village made the error of viewing the child as a responsible woman because she slept with a man.

The mother cries, the grandmother as well. The show is over. But the passions are not purged. The actors whose lives have just been enacted go back with their beliefs and hatreds, fired up by the exhibition.

A strange feeling that this "reality," because of its staging, was not true, in other words, that they never got to the truth of the people, or the story. What was certain, striking, was the fascination that incest held for all participants and the desire to put their victim, the beautiful little girl, to death.

Later I thought that there will be more and more reality shows, fiction will disappear, then we will no longer tolerate this dramatized reality and fiction will return.

May 29

Attack at the Uffizi Gallery in Florence. Five dead and paintings damaged, including one Giotto. Unanimous outcry: incalculable losses, irreparable. Not about the men, women, and baby who died, but about the paintings. Art is therefore more important than life, the representation of a fifteenth-century Madonna worth more than the body and breath of a child. Because the Madonna spanned centuries, and millions of visitors to the museum would still have had the pleasure of seeing her, whereas the child killed made only a very small number of people happy and he would have died one day anyway? But art is not something beyond humanity. In Giotto's Madonna, there was the flesh of the women that he met and touched. Between the death of a child and the destruction of his painting, what would he have chosen? We cannot be certain. His painting, perhaps. Thereby demonstrating the dark side of art.

June 17

Auchan, nine o'clock at night, in line at the cash. A guy, face flushed, continuously muttering about people who pay by check or by plastic, "can't have any money on them!" He is getting restless, "if they'd gotten up like me at four o'clock in the morning!" On the conveyor belt, he has placed a 1.5 liter plastic bottle of wine. This scene is out of place in the increasingly prim and proper Trois-Fontaines Shopping Center. Like with the beggar in the subway, people look elsewhere.

Always this feeling of cheating when I use a specialized word for the first time, today, *item*.

June 29

At eight in the morning the sun was already beating down on the windows of the RER. We were moving past huge mounds of sand and gravel, near l'Oise. A small restaurant-hotel, *Á la passerelle*, that looked old. In place of the former Nanterre shantytown, razed about ten years ago, is a Gypsy camp.

It was hot and the men stared openly at the women, as if in this sunshine the spontaneous erection of wake-up could not subside and the RER car were one big bed.

July 6

In the Trois-Fontaines Shopping Center, a video store has replaced Go Sport, which has moved next to Darty. Where the butcher Le boeuf limousin used to be, an Asian food counter — fish (that stank), Italian products — a cheese shop (that smelled good and strong), and a tobacco and news stand. On the two floors of Super-M, La Redoute, McD's, Etam, etc. have set up. Samaritaine has changed to Auchan, Bricogem has become Grand Optical, a kind of factory that manufactures glasses behind the counter while you wait. Rodier, Coryse Salomé, Kookaï have disappeared. A few very old institutions remain: Eram, Bata, André, Phildar Yarn and Socks, Singer sewing machines, "we taught the world to sew."

The sensation of time passing is not inside us. It comes from the outside, from children who grow up, neighbors who leave, from people growing older and dying. Bakeries that close and are replaced by driving schools or television repair shops. The cheese department moved to the back of the supermarket, which is no longer called Franprix but Leader Price.

July 12

Young musicians have gotten on at Sartrouville. They are playing *La foule, Mon amant de Saint-Jean*, melodies from a time before the RER and the new towns existed. I give them ten francs, as I give to anonymous figures and faces of misery. The same gesture to pay for pleasure or compassion.

Songs transform life into a novel. They render what we have experienced beautiful or faraway. The beauty later sets off the pain when we hear them again.

In Raymond Depardon's film about the asylum on San Clemente Island in Venice, we see a man collapsed on a table. A transistor glued to his ear, he is listening intently to a song. It is an Italian song reminiscent of fairgrounds, open air dances, lost love. The man listens and cries.

1993

August 3

At a slow cash at Auchan, a young mother with her small daughter. She comments aloud on the child's actions, "stop dragging your feet, you're wiping the entire floor with your dress!" She scolds her, "stay here!" Describes the immediate future to her, "we're going to heat the water to wash the dishes when we get home. You know there was no hot water this morning, Mommy had to take a cold shower." And so on. The little girl barely listens, repeats "cold shower" without conviction, as if she knew that her mother was playing to the crowd.

Behind them a group: a mother and well-behaved teenagers, suppressed laughter, controlled movements. Impossible to hear what they are saying. The shopping is assembled neatly on the belt: pretty notebooks, school supplies marked *Chevignon*, staples — UHT milk, yogurt, Nutella, pasta — neither vegetables nor meat, no doubt bought in specialty shops. A well-heeled family that does not need to be "noticed" and that draws its strength from its very invisibility.

August 12

People rush to the escalator leading down to the platform, at Auber. It glides along, packed with people. There is enough time to see, down below, along the blue wall, a couple hugging, kissing. Both in their forties. A train rumbles through. The man and the woman separate and run toward the train. They were at the spot where, one evening last year, toward midnight, I was with F. Like the woman, I had my back to the wall. The empty escalator had continued down, interminably, clicking continually.

August 13

In the "Avenir Secrétariat" copy center, the technician is making photocopies for an African. In the background, a young woman and two middle-aged women are in consultation, with amazing, identical smiles that seem as if they will never fade. It's their turn. They want wedding menus. The young woman holds the model they have prepared; the technician looks it over, impassively: "okay, on the same line or below?" They have her show them the various types of paper and sizes, look for a long while. The two who turn out to be the mother and the godmother let the girl choose, the future bride, then ask her insistently: "do you like it?" All three form a mass of softness, of loveliness, united as they wait and prepare for the "big day," like a century ago.

August 16

In the new town, near the RER station, a black woman in a light brown pleated skirt, beige blouse and round hat, like the ones Quakers wear. Leaning on the cement edge overlooking the tracks below, a girl, dressed in jeans and a parka, despite the heat, with a vague look on her face. Three girls, one of whom is carrying a bouquet of greenery, with their mother. A white man, in his fifties, short-sleeved shirt, knapsack, walks athletically. A group of men and women, young, same outfit, black pants and white shirts (a sect or salespeople from a store?), walks to the entrance of the RER.

Today, for a few minutes, I tried to *see* all the people I ran into, all strangers. It seemed to me that, as I observed these people in detail, their existence suddenly became very close to me, as if I were touching them. Were I to continue such an experiment, my vision of the world and of myself would turn out to be radically transformed. Perhaps I would disappear.

August 17

Nine o'clock in the morning, Auchan, when it opens, practically empty. As far as the eye can see, mounds of tomatoes, peaches, grapes — on parallel shelves, lit up, yogurt, cheeses, cold cuts. Strange sensation of beauty. I'm at the edge of Eden, seeing the first morning of the world. And EVERYTHING IS EDIBLE, or almost.

At the end, narrow aisles at the cash. When people go through there, things thrown haphazardly in the grocery carts seem small, not as pretty as in the abundance of the superstore, no different from those bought quickly at the Arab grocery on the corner.

August 25

Seeing PARIS written on a blue background, just as I was taking the road leading to Highway A15, suddenly filled me with astonishment, with happiness. For the first time, I was reading this name on the sign with my imagination at age fifteen, when I had never yet gone to Paris, when that city was a dream. A rare moment, when the sensation of the past recurs in the present, superimposes itself. As when making love, when all the men past and the one who is there are but one.

August 31

In the afternoon, at the entrance to Place des Touleuses, an old woman is leaning up against a wall. Around her, a group of people, many children. She begins to walk, slowly, dazed, supported on each side by a woman and a man who shouts angrily to the crowd, "I'm not a nurse!" Children are running around shouting, exclaiming. She is a bit hunched over, dressed in gray, with gray hair, glasses. Blood trickles from her swollen nose. She holds her purse on her forearm tucked against her stomach.

Accompanied by the little group leading her to the doctor's office, she crosses the deserted square that is white with sun like sand in a bullring.   1993

September 1

A mother and daughter are walking along the subway platform, the daughter clinging to her mother's arm. A gesture of times past, from the country: girls who walked along the main street like that, on Sundays, to protect themselves from the world and the groups of boys hanging out in front of the movie theater.

September 10

At Trois-Fontaines, a couple alone on the escalator going up. From below, only the boy's back is visible. They are hugging each other close, rubbing up against one another. From time to time, the boy turns his head, looks at the people further down with their grocery carts. They appear to be rising toward the sky. The boy's shirt is bright red.

Today at noon. I am sitting in the living room, eyes closed. I hear cars going by on the wet road below. A truck. I picture the sloping garden, the white fence, the street. In my head a sentence forms, "the constant hum of cars, and the longer sound of tires screeching on the damp pavement," with which surely I will do nothing. Simple habit of putting the world into words.

"I am going to take *my* RER." A way of describing the link and the familiarity with things that we use regularly. *My* RER: Line A, that takes me to Paris, always brings me back to the same Cergy-Préfecture station, where I board without thinking and know all the stops without needing to look at the signs on the platforms. Where I feel I belong among the crowds of users of this line, this community of anonymous people for whom it is also *their* RER.

The RER of lines B, C and D are not mine (nor the cars of Line A RER that head toward the ritzy suburbs — Le Pecq, Saint-Germain-en-Laye). Imperceptibly, I feel strange there, practically an intruder.

October 28

Two women got on at Parc-des-Expositions. Sitting across from one another. One young, dark and pretty, one blond, about fifty, slouching a bit in her seat. From the aggressive tone of voice of the young one, it is a mother and daughter. "Are you taking us out to eat this evening?" The mother hesitates: "No . . . We have to go to . . . (inaudible)." The girl, gleefully: "You see! You're not being honest. You only had to say so right away!" The mother is silent.

The daughter continues: "Françoise asked me what you wanted for your birthday: a blouse, is that okay?"

"Yes, yes."

"I wasn't going to say that you wanted, I don't know, a Chanel suit!" (The girl's sarcastic laughter).

The mother tries to mollify her daughter: "That's nice of you" and sets off a new explosion of irony from her daughter: "Of course it's nice!"

All the way to Gare du Nord, each sentence the mother says — forcing herself to maintain a neutral tone — is picked apart by the daughter, who immediately detects a hidden meaning, the true meaning: the mother's nastiness. "See what you're like!" The mother's words are examined microscopically and condemned by the daughter with a relentlessness that would inspire terror, were it not perceived as a sign of malaise, of boredom, resolved in facile persecution, and going unpunished by the woman who brought her into the world.

November 12

A voice sounds in the RER: "I'm unemployed. I'm living in a hotel with my wife and child, we have twenty-five francs to live on a day." What follows is the story of ordinary poverty, repeated probably ten times an hour, in the same tone of voice. The man is selling *Le Réverbère*, a newspaper. The words express humility, "I'm not asking a lot from you, just a bit of small change to help me." He makes his way through the car. No one buys the newspaper. When it comes time to get out, the man shouts threateningly: "Have a great day and a good weekend!" No one looks up. The irony of poor people does not count; it's not a weapon, just an annoyance.

November 16

In *Le Monde*, the following headline: "The International War Crimes Tribunal not Backed by Real Political Will."

Forty thousand documents exist on the acts of violence committed in Bosnia. "Four hundred concentration and detention camps, ninety-eight common graves containing almost three thousand bodies, and three thousand victims of rape have already been counted. But, according to Mr. Bassioni, the risk of losing evidence increases with time. Loss of evidence is one of our main concerns."

I write that, and everything I write here, as *evidence*.

November 21

Book Fair of the Pen Club, in the lobby of the Maison de la radio. Minks, jewelry, on women who all have the same look — older women trying to appear young: slim, flat-chested, vaporous blonds, pretty teeth and wrinkled faces. "Dear friend, thank you for coming." The writer of exotic novels gets up this way several times, stretching arms out over his stack of books to elegantly greet his acquaintances. It appears that the Pen Club was created to come to the aid of imprisoned writers, subjected to torture.

On the platform at Étoile station a clown arrives, very thin, with a small leather briefcase. He paces up and down the platform, shading his eyes with his hands,

"I'm looking for my audience." Surprise, embarrassment of those waiting for the RER. He sets down his briefcase, takes out a red McD's tray that he sets on the ground. In a split second, his legs are around his neck; he is walking on his hands the length of the platform, threading his way like a large beetle between the people, whom he shouts at with a mixture of aggressiveness and kindness. In front of one girl, he thunders, "I'm going to jump over!" No, Miss, not you, the railing!" and he leaps onto the row of seats. To one man, "Eh! You've never made love like that!" Little by little, people loosen up, relax their bodies that turn and now follow the convolutions of the clown on the platform. People hear only him; his voice resonates in the half-deserted Sunday station. He is a large worm wriggling on the ground. He unfolds himself abruptly and takes out a toy gun to force people to give him money. People laugh. Is it sad or happy — hard to say.

November 22

On *France Inter*, on the radio, this morning:

Six people, including three teenagers and a little girl, died in a working class area in Mulhouse, on rue de la Fabrique: Turks, who were living in an attic. A wood stove seems to have caused the fire.

Two homeless people have died of the cold, one at Mureaux in Yvelines, the other in La Rochelle.

According to the Prime Minister, "the economy seems to be getting onto the right track again."

Welcome to the world of Rhône-Poulenc. For one hundred and thirty-francs, become a shareholder, etc. (A man's voice, ingratiating.)

Your work is the most important thing for you. Why would someone HIV-positive be any different from you? (A man's voice, masculine and full of conviction).

November 25

Boulevard Saint-Germain is deserted smack in the middle of the afternoon. Coming from Saint-Michel, the first lines of demonstrators with white banners appear. The stores on the boulevard have lowered their shutters. Canal 127, a clothing boutique that had remained open, lowers its shutters hastily. The saleswomen remain in the background, in their fashionable clothing, watching the crowd that all looked the same in their jeans and jackets, high school students.

November 27

A woman's voice. "You like to be popular, loved. Why would a person with HIV be any different from you? You can kiss him, go out to eat with him, etc." Morality comes from the radio, through ads.

December 1

"AIDS Day." Fourteen million HIV-positive people in the world. In Paris, almost all people with AIDS are cremated, like the plague victims of long ago.

Condoms are a franc apiece in all pharmacies. An attractive price. But not the place: always the white blouse on the other side of the counter, inquiring: "what would you like?" To answer: "two condoms," is to confess in a pharmacy, before everyone, that you are going to make love. Only vending machines liberate.

1993

1994

February 6

A mortar bomb exploded today, Sunday, on the main marketplace in Sarajevo. Sixty-two people are dead, more than two hundred wounded.

People cannot talk about or describe that, even in a tone of outrage. The only answer would be if all the people in France and Europe assembled in the squares and demanded that governments find a solution to the conflict. If we do not do that, it is because this war and these children killed on the marketplace of Sarajevo are less important to us than the lottery, the movie playing on TV in the evening, they are just tragic background noise. "We are gripped by shame," certain intellectuals claim. They are mistaken; distant reality does not make people feel ashamed.

February 8

Evening at Châtelet-Les-Halles. A man selling *Le Monde* feverishly paces up and down the platform, looking determined, or desperate, saying in a monotone voice, "*Le Monde*, buy *Le Monde*," among the foreign words, a leitmotif.

An African with a guitar sings a very long monotonous chant in French about his childhood in Mali, his mother, the hut, traditions. A white woman accompanies him, on guitar as well; she is not singing. People gather round them little by little, coming to catch the music, the words from a past that isn't theirs, for the most part, but that speaks to them of childhood, of a lost country.

In the RER, in big letters on the page of the newspaper a man is reading, SEE-THROUGH PANTYHOSE ARE COMING BACK.

March 18

At the top of the escalator, at Les Halles, a man was begging. Protruding slightly from his pants, cut off at the knees, were the stumps of his amputated legs. They looked like the tips of two huge penises.

At Montparnasse Station, an invisible accordion was playing *Il est revenu le temps du muguet* and the tune of *Les Parapluies de Cherbourg*. At the bend in a corridor, a group of ticket inspectors in brown uniforms, four or five lined up along the wall and four others, surrounded and harshly questioned a man. He was young, with dark skin, hair in a ponytail. Overwhelming feeling of the *order of things*.

Sadness and dejection of people selling newspapers in the street now. The novelty of this help to the home-less has faded. More and more, these charity newspa-pers — which no one considers as "real" newspapers, nor selling them as "real" work — appear like a pathetic means to accommodate poverty, even prevent it from becoming dangerous.

March 31

A figure appeared suddenly before me as I was weed-ing my garden path. I looked up. It was a short, stout woman, about sixty, dressed simply in warm clothes. She smiled. "Excuse me for disturbing you. Have you seen a large, black cat, by any chance? I left him with someone in the La Justice area who let him run away."

I told her that I had only seen one black and white cat, yesterday. She remained there. I suggested that she go look in the shed; the cupboard beneath the roof there often served as a shelter to stray cats. Inside the shed, I asked her the name of her cat, to call him. She laughed gently, "we call him Pépère." I didn't dare shout "Pépère!" — just banged on the cupboard with my fist. There was no cat. We went back down the path in silence. Then, hesitantly: "They told me he would come back on his own. Pointoise is far from here, though . . ." I advised her to telephone the SPCA. "Yes, but he isn't tattooed . . ." She was still smiling gently; she didn't seem to want to leave.

It really is spring. All the trees are in bloom.

April 18

Auber. Right at the spot where the moving sidewalks start, a man who has lost both his legs is begging. I wonder if he's the same one as at Les Halles. Stepping onto the moving sidewalk, I look at him from behind. It seems to me I see his legs folded beneath his buttocks.

April 27

In Maisons-Alfort, in Les Juilliottes, I found that long street again, the one whose name I don't know that runs from Avenue Général-Leclerc to Avenue Léon-Blum. I took it five or six times to go to Doctor M. To the right, I saw the suburban homes again — some of which had always seemed to me to be abandoned and that today had their shutters open; to the left buildings, the huge parking lot. A bulldozer was leveling the public gardens, perhaps to construct other buildings. After the tax office, I smelt the usual sickeningly sweet aroma, probably from a chemical company. Toward the end of the street, where it narrows, more small houses, an off-track betting café, a company that installs windshields, a house with shutters closed behind a grille. There were second-generation North African women, Beurettes, in groups of two or three — it's a holiday and the weather's good. I began to like this rue de Maisons-Alfort, in a suburb I don't know.

May 5

In a corridor at Bastille station, these words in enormous letters, in chalk, on the ground: FOR FOOD. A little further on, in the same way: THANK YOU. Further still, kneeling down right in the middle of the corridor, the man who wrote it, a cup at the end of his extended hand. The wave of people parts into two streams before him. I was in the one to the right.

May 17

The French teacher at the high school in A., in the North, who teaches an "underprivileged class," drives around in a Mercedes, jewelry, fashionable scarf, a reserved blond. The fact that she was born in a working-class milieu, as she proclaims, does not alter the fact that for the students: she is *now* a bourgeoise. Everything she says in class against advertising, money as king, holds no weight against the obscene vision of a Mercedes parked in front of Lycée Guy-Mollet.

May 26

On the billboards the beautiful woman with the serious face has reappeared, sleek hair pulled into a low bun. She uncovers a breast completely by raising it slightly as if preparing to breastfeed. But the somewhat collapsed breast is that of a mature woman who has cancer. The woman's eyes meet that of other women everywhere, in the subway, in the street.

One day note all the posters pasted on the walls of several subway stations, with their slogans. To determine exactly the imaginary reality, fears, and desires of the moment. The signs of present history that memory does not retain — or judges to be unworthy of retaining.

July 21

We are walking on a long, very straight bridle path, the end of which we do not see, in the L'Isle-Adam Forest. Three women arrive from the opposite direction. Two young women and one older, perhaps their mother, with branches in their hands. We ask them where this path leads. "Nowhere," they say, rather distractedly, exclaiming together immediately, triumphantly: "THERE'S AN EXHIBITIONIST!" It appears that a middle-aged man, wearing a blue leather sweater, followed them throughout their walk, hiding in the bushes. The girls are martially brandishing the sticks they picked up to protect themselves. All in all, according to their description, it does not seem that the man is exhibiting his penis. He is more of a furtive watcher that the great shadowy forest produced for an afternoon of lawless desire. The brush with danger overexcites the three girls, still agitated by this encounter in the woods where they experienced something of the ancestral hunt, the wild eyes of the male tracking the female through the foliage.

November 15

The cashiers at Auchan say hello at the exact moment when, having given the previous customer the receipt, they plunk your first item on the conveyor belt. Try as we may to place ourselves in their field of vision, right across from them, sometimes for more than five minutes, it is only at that moment when they begin to ring up our purchases that they seem to discover us. This strange and ritual blindness reveals that they are only obeying a requirement forcing them to be polite. From the viewpoint of marketing, we only exist at the moment when containers of detergent and yogurt are exchanged for money.

The hope, always in vain, of having nothing more to note, to no longer be swallowed up by anything whatsoever in this world, by the wave of anonymous people that I encounter and of which, for the others, I am a part.

December 2

For the meeting with Taslima Nasreen, at the Pompidou Center, no one may enter without an invitation that must be shown along with an identification card. Also, purses must be opened. This rigorous inspection appears to amuse the crowd of guests, happy to momentarily attain the status of dangerous individuals. People sit down in the room, chatting and laughter continue. Being forbidden to leave before the end excites them a great deal, "Are you hungry? Too bad for you! You know we're shut in!" An increasingly strong and delicious sensation of imagining oneself in danger.

The people who are to question Taslima Nasreen enter and sit down at a table, on the stage, facing the public. French women writers, an Iranian, two men. Here is Taslima Nasreen, tall, beautiful, and calm, in Bengali dress. She sits down. A man crouches down behind her, her translator. The first woman writer who speaks is impassioned, describes to Taslima Nasreen that around us, everywhere here, are hundreds of paintings, of books. Taslima Nasreen reads a declaration in English that writer Leslie Kaplan begins to translate. Someone, in the room, interrupts her, roundly criticizes her translation and declares that there's no point in translating English; "everyone understands it." The people in the room seem in agreement. I wonder if I am the only one who doesn't understand everything.

The women and men at the table are now questioning Taslima Nasreen on her vocation as writer, on writing. Her answers seem disjointed, perhaps due to the translation, and contrived. From the audience, a few people ask her questions; does she think there is such a thing as a feminine practice of writing. She replies that women are more observant than men; they must find their own language, and that that is not feminist but humanist. It is a ceremony where it is important that all participants feel they are playing a role. For many spectators, that consists of criticizing the questions asked by others. Perhaps it would be better not to break the contemplation of this woman threatened by death who is taken around from country to country like a statue of the Virgin to give those who look at her the impression that they are doing something for freedom.

December 16

At the Café Flore, a man is speaking to a woman who is in constant agreement. His loud and passionate voice fills the terrace. "I don't want to listen to a woman twenty-four hours a day, be her protector!" he says. Becoming more and more worked up: "I'd also like to be a child, a wild animal acting on its urges!" More calmly, in a dreamy tone of voice, "I want to be able to leave when I want. A bit like a cat, see?" The conversation now focuses on the feminine and masculine part of each individual, a theory that the man explains to his companion as if it were a personal idea he had just discovered. He proclaims that it's good to be with a "cerebral woman, a bit masculine." She agrees.

They exchange phone numbers. They get up and leave. She is young, very beautiful. He, middle-aged, and seems very hip. Perhaps he takes himself for Sartre who was in the habit of seducing young and pretty women in this café.

1995

January 13

The young blond woman who rushed into the RER without letting the passengers exit is sitting across from me with a bag of chips. Periodically, not rushing, she dips her hand into the package, takes out a chip, crunches it. I would like her to finish quickly. The slowness and tranquility with which she crunches her chips make my heart speed. I become increasingly annoyed. I think I could kill her — and even that would not be enough, torture her perhaps — like those teenagers who obey only their desires, who suddenly raise their fist or take a knife to a stranger whose "face they don't like."

January 14

Jeanne Calment, the oldest woman in the world, will celebrate her one hundred and twentieth birthday next month. Her doctor speaks of her, describes her quick retorts, emphasizes her vivaciousness and humor, has many anecdotes about her performances. At one hundred years old she did this, and one hundred and ten that: "Can you imagine that I found her one day replacing a light bulb in her dining room chandelier , perched on a footstool atop the table!" It seems she is receiving hundreds of letters of congratulations for her birthday. As if this long life were an accomplishment. But Jeanne Calment did nothing other than fulfill, in complete indifference, her genetic destiny.

For several centuries, the western world has become accustomed to measuring human life in terms of nature, rocks and trees, meditating upon the ruins and dusty shadows that prey on them. Each summer millions of tourists come to find again traces of the past in the châteaux of the Loire Valley and on the Pont du Gard. But nothing can compare to the feeling experienced by seeing a living being, a body carrying an unprecedented number of years. We would like to keep this shrunken, wrinkled body, but that is the same as that of the little girl running in the streets of Arles in the 1880s.

January 20

Jacques Gaillot was a guest on the show *Nulle part ailleurs* on Canal+ last evening. All around, hosts and guests showered him with obscene laughter and jokes. He said nothing, smiled naively. He looked like a Good Angel thrown in among wild and lewd devils. So much innocence — we can imagine him smiling in the same way in the worst of Sade's castles — has something worrisome — or constructed about it.

January 25

We see a couple. He is in an armchair, in his fifties, has myopathy. She is beside him, heavy, maternal. A doctor is speaking to them. The man has decided to die with the help of the doctor when the deterioration becomes unbearable. Awaiting that moment, the doctor visits the couple regularly, in the little house. They speak warmly.

"The moment has come," the man says. The protocol unfolds: the first injection will put him to sleep, the second will stop his heart. The wife looks on attentively, comments. When it's all over, she cries. She goes to fetch the last letter her husband wrote her the day before, a few sentences that had cost him six hours of effort and pain. This takes place in the Netherlands.

A terrible scene to see, because of its simplicity, because of its *gentleness*. Death here is no longer a scandal, a violent tearing away from the world and from human beings. It is a thing looked at calmly, by the doctor, the wife, observing the effects of the injections. And by the cameraman, about whom nothing is said. This film forces us to picture a world where, in a way, the choice of death is part of life's plans, where "doing away with oneself" is an option as thinkable as marrying.

March

The children of Sarajevo, orphans among the ruins. There is Mario. He says, "at night, I dream that my mother is alive." He is wearing a hat pulled down to his eyes, is smiling. The television makes him radiant, as if he were in a stained glass window.

May 16

Television. A small group of people, scattered, rue Saint-Honoré, in front of the Élysée Palace. Men and women, children, each carrying a rose. They enter the courtyard of the Élysée, undecided, intimidated. Danielle Mitterrand appears, has them advance to the steps. François Mitterrand suddenly appears. "Don't stay there; it's cold," he says, waving them a welcome like someone receiving unexpected guests. They slowly enter with their roses standing straight up, like candles. It is François Mitterrand's last day as President of the Republic.

Tears come to me. With this man who has just said "don't stay there" like an old country gentleman on the steps of his house, fourteen years of my life are over.

May 20

Near Place de l'Alma, on a median dividing the road, a man is lying on the ground, huddled up. Cars pass. An old woman crosses a lane, passes close to the sleeping man and glances at him but doesn't stop. So he isn't dead.

At Stalingrad Station, a quivering package of blankets gets on the subway. In the middle of the fabric, the wrinkled face of an old Arab carrying his bedding around his head and shoulders. He looks like a Bedouin who has lost his caravan, swaying between Stalingrad and Barbès.

June 6

On the radio: "The President of the Republic has telephoned Boris Yeltsin." For a few seconds, we still see François Mitterrand.

The same evening, President Chirac is on TV, pronouncing the eulogy of a soldier from UNPROFOR killed in Sarajevo. He reads, hammering out each word forcefully, a short text, on several sheets that he slides regularly one beneath the others. Mechanically, he looks up between each word. He does not yet know how to *appear* moved, revealing that now he is between two activities and is seeing the speech, written by a secretary, for the first time. The UNPROFOR soldier was twenty-two years old.

More and more homeless people selling *La Rue*, *Le Réverbère*, etc., everywhere, in the subway, at the doors of superstores, at red lights in the rain. The cars do not lower their windows. These are "homeless newspapers," not real newspapers.

In the RER, a newspaper vendor has just got off when another gets on. "Hello, my name is Éric, I'm out of work; if you'd like to help me by buying *La Rue*." Always the voice first, straining to stop conversations, to make people look up. The face scans the car rather quickly, trying to make eye contact, or not, depending on the degree of fatigue or disillusion. This one is a boy in glasses, wearing a raincoat despite the heat. I have a son called Éric.

Early July

At Thilliers-en-Vexin, on the highway from Paris to Rouen, written on the wall of a large house on a street corner, at the traffic lights: CUCKOLDED, in huge letters. The anonymous author wanted hundreds of drivers, stopping at the red light, to read the sign of infamy, the understatement destined to kill. Experiencing a two-fold delight: having a wide public, constantly renewed, and remaining hidden behind his work. Perhaps the intended recipient of this anachronistic insult lives here, not daring to erase what will bloom again the following night.

First decree by a mayor forbidding begging and "lying down" in public. This was bound to happen. So we can finally hide those people who exhibit their shape- less bodies, near the unfashionable bottle of cheap red wine, the sight of which offends tourists seated at café terraces.

"Lying down," the position of love, sleep, and death. Of abandonment and time stopped. A vision that denies civilization and progress. Temptation.

The Serbs have recaptured Srebenica, Zepa. As no one now is able to imagine a *real* war, nor the *current* concentration camps, everyone becomes indignant and couldn't care less.

July 26

Yesterday a bomb exploded in the RER, at Saint-Michel station. It was five-thirty in the evening. Seven dead, and people wounded whose legs were blown off. These underground places where crowds gather are ideal for bomb attacks, a drop of acid thrown into a hive of activity. We don't know yet all the names of those who died at Saint-Michel. In a week, in a month, we'll be waiting on that platform where bodies were pulverized as if nothing had happened.

December 24

Today, Christmas Eve, returning from the fish market, I gave ten francs to a man collapsed near the garbage bags, at the top of the filthy steps leading down to the RER station. A face ravaged by poverty and alcohol. He smelled very bad. "Happy Christmas!" he cried. I replied mechanically: "you too." Afterwards I was so disgusted with myself that to erase the shame, I wanted to wrap myself up in his coat, kiss his hands, smell his breath.

1996

Early January

They have found the body of Céline Figard, the nine-teen-year-old who disappeared in England more than a week ago. According to the autopsy, she was not killed immediately after her disappearance. She was sequestered for several days before being finished off by her murderer, perhaps the long distance truck driver who picked her up at the highway rest area where she was hitch hiking. This lapse of time between the moment when the disappearance was noted and when she was killed, those few days when she was *still* alive, is the most tragic element of this news item. Her family will always have in their minds those days when the girl was somewhere in England, hoping for her release, that time when they could have done something. This impossibility of going back to those days and changing the course of things is the horror of existence. There was also a time in Chile, in Argentina, in Rwanda, when men and women, in prisons, were *still* alive.

January 11

At the Mobil service station, in the afternoon, an employee about twenty years old is at the cash listening to the radio. I am the only customer. Distractedly he takes my debit card, inserts it in the machine, a smile floating on his lips. It is *Les grosses têtes*, on Radio-Télévision Luxembourg. The radio host is addressing a female listener, "so you would agree that we should use the exact words, I don't know, for instance, e-ja-cu-la-tion?" "Yes, yes, but not too much, of course . . ." The host bursts out laughing: "You're right, when there's too much, it spills over everywhere!" Laughter from the show's audience and the host's buddies. I punch in the code of my credit card and wait in front of the counter for the employee to detach the slip. He gives it to me without looking at me, beaming, lost in delight more obscene than the words on the radio.

January 13

Politicians, and subsequently journalists, use terms like "colloquium," "summit," puffing up these empty words to give them importance. They make a point of articulating very clearly: "there appears to be," and emphasize every syllable: "we are continuing to experience." This politico-media pronunciation resembles that of grade school teachers reading a dictation to their students. Chirac, Juppé, and the others seem to want to educate the people, teach them spelling and proper use of language.

January 19

A story to enact, one already dating from last year.

You place a pair of shoes on the ground, in front of the audience, ankle boots, if possible. Slide a lit cigarette inside a shoe, having been careful to take a good drag in order to produce abundant smoke. The audience is then greeted with the view of a pair of shoes from which smoke escapes and you ask: "what is it?" Hesitation in the audience, nervous laughter. Then you say, "this is a guy who was waiting for the bus in Sarajevo." This story creates great mirth, provided it is set up: it is absolutely essential to see the shoe from which the thin wreaths emerge. In one second — the time needed for a grenade — we *see* the man vanish into thin air, ruins, the pair of shoes change into a hideous symbol. We cannot endure such a metaphor without howling with laughter.

Writing this story is perhaps not the worst way of not forgetting the war in Bosnia.

Early May

The concourse of the train station leads underground to where the buses stop. Set back a little, a harshly-lit snack bar sells sandwiches and drinks. At the foot of an escalator that is almost always out of order, Africans are offering posters for sale. Cans of beer on the ground. Imperceptibly, Cergy-Préfecture station has begun to resemble, on a small scale, all the stations of the world where there are a lot of people: Marseilles, Vienna, Bratislava. Where a girl sits at the far end of a snack bar in the afternoon.

On the wall of the train station parking lot, the graffiti, in English: *If your children are happy they are communists*, etc., is beginning to fade. *Elsa I love you* has disappeared. There is still *Algeria I love you*, splattered with blood.

May 10

For several weeks, the mouse lived behind the stove, accumulating provisions — the cat's kibble — and setting down clumps of a sort of yellowish wool, a future nest. An odor of urine was given off as soon as the stove was turned on. She resisted all efforts to make her leave. Each night, she would bring back the provisions and

the wool that I removed in the daytime. To put an end
to it, the evening before last, I set a trap. She devoured
the cheese without releasing the spring. So much intel-
ligence should have been rewarded but I carried on
regardless, set up the mechanism again. This morning I
found her strangled by the mousetrap around her body,
her head on the side, her eyes open.

I removed the little body from the mousetrap and
threw it in the garbage. I cleaned one last time beneath
the stove, collected the wool and bits of food. I had
become accustomed to her being there. When I used the
stove, when I turned on the oven, I knew she was there,
hidden underneath, listening out for all the sounds,
recognizing them, perfectly adapted to her life in my
stove. Even the heat from the oven must no longer have
impressed her. I broke a tie involving life.

June 12

At Leclerc, in the vegetable department, the smell of
bleach, overpowering, like that of sperm.

August

Boris Yeltsin has taken an oath on the Constitution. A
five-minute ceremony. The leader of the second world
power appears virtually silent, bloated, and moves along
in fits and starts. It seems that a stone statue has come
in his place.

To P., vaguely reproving, who asks her why she plays the lottery, his mother replies "it's just to have something to wait for."

December 13

The subway car is full. A woman's voice is raised, powerful. "Act a little human!" Absolute silence. A terrible voice, that tells of her misfortune, accuses people of selfishness, their asses nice and warm, etc. No one looks at her or responds to her anger, because she is telling the truth. On the platform, she collides with people carrying bags of Christmas presents, hurls abuse at them, "you'd be better off giving money to the unfortunate rather than buying all that crap." Again the truth. But we do not give to do good, we give to be loved. Giving to a homeless person just to prevent him from dying altogether is an intolerable idea and it would not make him love us anyway.

1997

At Châtelet, I was preparing to get off, when a woman asked in a loud voice "to take the RER, it's at Les Halles, not here?" I told her she could reach it by Châtelet. On the platform, she headed in the opposite direction; I motioned to her to come back. It was at that moment, or a few seconds later, that a woman's voice came from the loudspeaker: FOLLOWING . . . (she hesitated) A SIG-NIFICANT EMISSION OF SMOKE, WE ASK PASSENGERS TO GET OFF THE TRAIN AND HEAD TOWARDS THE EXIT.

It seems to me that I thought, "this is happening to me" and "being there *at just that moment*." We all walked toward the exit, at the back. The woman on the loud-speaker repeated that we should stay CALM AND COOL as we headed for the exit. Her voice was trembling. At the end of the platform, the exit I was intending to take — Place Sainte-Opportune — was blocked by police officers who directed us to another corridor. It was full of smoke. I moved forward in terror, trying not to breathe. The calm of the crowd was impressive. I felt my body ready to charge, to shove people. Inter-minable minutes before we got out. On the sidewalk, at the entrance to the station, a fire truck was parked. People gathered there asked me what was happening. I didn't answer; I walked rapidly, not thinking, down rue de Rivoli, telling myself that people didn't know there was an attack at Châtelet, the dead and wounded were already covered by life, like at Saint-Michel and Port-Royal. Then I remembered that I was supposed to go to Opéra, which meant I'd need to take a bus. Slowly I emerged from my state; probably there had been no attack, just a fire. Later, I thought with amaze-ment about that woman I had been for an hour.

January 11

Leclerc. At the cash, a tall young man, face full of acne, has finished placing his purchases that have been rung up into his shopping cart. When it comes time to pay, he doesn't say a word and looks over the heads of the customers, toward the inside of the store, thus indicating he is waiting for someone — his wife, no doubt — who has the money. Everyone is waiting. The usual gestures of annoyance. The cashier grabs hold of the telephone, "order on hold." A bit later an employee arrives who carries out a procedure on the cash with a key. The cashier goes on to the next customer. The young man abandons his shopping cart and goes back inside the store, returns to the cash, watching, impassive, for the woman who does not appear. The cashier has kept on giving him dirty looks, staring, as she rings up the next customer's purchases. When she has finished, she gets up, ostensibly goes to fetch the full shopping cart, abandoned, pushes it to one side, sits down again, and rings up my purchases. The young man can no longer be seen, lost in the aisles in search of the woman. When I've finished paying, and push my shopping cart toward the exit, the young man has resurfaced, alone, turning his head in all directions, still with a strange impassivity. Perhaps his wife is trying on a pair of pants in a changing room, or reading in the book department. Or else she is playing hide and seek, enjoying shaking him off between the gardening products and the dog food, to laugh or avenge herself and humiliate him in front of everyone. Or she has chosen this moment to leave him, taking away the money and the car keys. Or simply she met another man and they are kissing in the cafeteria, making love in the washroom. The interpretations of reality are practically infinite.

February 17

Apparently forty-five per cent of people think it is good that there are members of the National Front in the Assembly.

February 20

Brunot Megret, on the radio, on Europe 1: "Our ideas are becoming widespread among the French population; we don't need to have fifteen members."

Fifty-nine per cent of people approve of the Debré Law that would make any immigrant a suspect who could be expelled on the slightest pretext.

February 22

We arrived at Gare de l'Est for the demonstration against the Debré Law at two o'clock. Hardly any more activity than on an ordinary Saturday but hordes of interviewers from market research companies await people at the subway exit. "Are you going to demonstrate? Would you like to complete this survey?" People complete it, placing the sheet against a café window. We walk down the Boulevard de Magenta, to the Da Mimo Restaurant, the meeting place given by SOS Racisme, with the filmmakers who are demonstrating. They are still eating, creating lots of noise. We leave again, head back toward Gare de l'Est, to the meeting place with the demonstrating writers, in front of the Monument to the Deported. No one is there. Too early, no doubt. Later people arrive who all kiss one another, including a tall, bald guy, with a wide-brimmed hat, very much the artist. In the middle of the station the writers begin to form a group, huddled-up against one another, shoulder to shoulder, showing only their backs. It seems as if force would be required to undo it. A second group forms in the same way. Contrary to cocktail parties where they circulate with ease, gliding smoothly from one point in the living room to another, looking forward, the writers in this concourse of Gare de l'Est pull together, opening their circle only to arrivals recognized as their own, with great exclamations.

At three o'clock, when we leave the station, people have invaded Boulevard de Magenta. We have lost the group of writers moved to the front line of the demonstration and find ourselves in the midst of the anonymous crowd. We all walk until six in the evening in the sunshine and warmth, between sidewalks jammed with people. The only action, at this very moment, consists of *being there*, of our presence, the group transformed into an idea that could modify the course of events. The *proof* of the idea's existence depended on this presence or physical absence—"hardly a soul" or a sea of people. It was a sea.

February 28

A loud voice in the RER. "I'm not selling newspapers today; I was, but no one is interested anymore." The man continues talking about all the people who marched in the streets to protest the Debré Law, but no one is marching against unemployment, "we can just keep on sleeping in the street and starving." Once again, the voice from below speaks the truth. With violence: "In 89, they cut off the king's head; people nowadays would be too scared to do that." All the while, I am correcting student essays on *Dom Juan*. The man speaking is poorer and more miserable than a peasant in Molière's day.

I didn't give him any money. Later an accordionist came by playing Dalida tunes. Irresistibly prompted to search for a coin in my purse. As if pleasure were more of an incentive to give than the naked sight of need.

March 4

On the radio, Alain Madelin was answering questions from listeners, who were saying: Salaries are going down, my pension is going down, I have no more work, Renault has just cut jobs. To each caller, Madelin invariably replied, "you have to create a company!" He separated the syllables slowly, pronouncing it "cre-ate:" you have to cre-ate! Cre-ate! In the tone of someone speaking to imbeciles. Triumphantly berating his listener: "I hear fear in your words, Sir!" A person must indeed be a total coward to not create a company when he is unemployed, with two months rent owed and the threat of property seizure.

At one point, Madelin flaunted his origins: "my father was an unskilled worker; I know what payslips are." As if he were the same as that boy of long ago, in a housing development.

This chatter, an insult to people and to reason, was uttered by a former minister in the government, with no one intervening to expose the contempt and insincerity. The listeners had no opportunity to "insult" him in return — for risk of the microphone being cut off — by asking how much he earned a month, where he lived, what company he himself had "cre-ated." Once again, the media legitimized the suggestions, however absurd, of an authoritative voice. I felt hatred (which is why I am writing these lines).

March 5

Gabrielle Russier committed suicide on September 1, 1969, at age thirty-two. She had been imprisoned for having loved one of her students, eighteen years old, a "minor" at that time. Cayatte made a film about it with Annie Girardot in the role of Gabrielle Russier, *Mourir d'aimer — To Die of Love*, with a song by Charles Aznavour. She did not die of love, but from having violated the foundations of the society that 68 had just shaken up. The family, first of all: divorced, she snatched a young man — the son of university professors — from his planned future, studies, middle-class marriage. A mother of two children, she flouted the role and "high-est mission" of a woman through this liaison with a young man. Then the school: a teacher, she transgressed the boundary between teachers and students, displaying the hidden relationship of desire between the two. In the end, the law arrived on the scene, carried out the wishes of the families and the school. Gabrielle Russier is an expiatory victim of 68, a kind of a modern-day saint.

March 7

The closing of the Renault factories in Vilvorde, Bel-guim, leads to the first European strike. At the same time, the Stock Exchange continues to fly high (the image itself is charming, light, while the words for the unemployed are heavy: "hit," "threatened"). To put it plainly, this means that men are let go so that others, the shareholders, will grow wealthy. Ultimately, the death of some could be accepted so that others may profit. They show us laid off workers, never the shareholders, invisible like the money.

In Cuba, children rent their toys to other children.

April 2

This afternoon, for an hour, Laetitia, a student, de-scribed on the radio, on France Inter, her work at "Le Téléphone Rose." Married men call during office hours; single men in the evening and on weekends. It is especially busy on Valentine's Day and New Year's Eve, because they can't stand being alone on those days. Laetitia makes them believe she is phoning from her home (which allows her to cut short the session by saying that the mailman is ringing the doorbell), that she does it for pleasure, not for money, and they like to believe her: "You're such a slut!" They respect their wives, who refuse sodomy and fellatio to the bitter end. All assure her that their penis measures at least eight and a half inches when erect and I don't remember how much in circumference. They say "listen to my dick." Nice.

April 24

Vincent Van Gogh, in a letter: "I seek to find a way to express the desperately swift passing away of things in modern life."

June 2

At the École normale supérieure on rue d'Ulm, a Czech professor, about forty years old, is waiting in the hallway: he is going to give a lecture. His anxiety is visible. We enter the room, about ten people. He begins to read his text, his voice trembling slightly. He is wearing a handsome green suit, with matching shirt and tie. So much anxiety, insomnia perhaps, for an hour of thoughts disseminated to ten folks, certain of whom, as usual, only take notes to prepare their offensive against the speaker. For the professor, for us who listen to him, wavering back and forth between interest and boredom on this warm day, this is a kind of *sacrifice* offered in the name of knowledge, wisdom.

June 18

From the baby carriage to the grave, life unfolds more and more between the shopping center and the television set. This is no more strange or absurd than life in days gone by in fields and cafés, or at evening gatherings.

August 5

The one hundred and twenty-two year old woman, humanity's most senior citizen, Jeanne Calment, has died. Almost national mourning. Of her life, she leaves no testimony likely to be universally conveyed, not even a diary. Her only achievement was living a life that continued beyond all expectations. Jeanne Calment was just time, the very incarnation of time.

Time that we did not experience. Her existence went back to where neither our memory nor that of our parents or even our grandparents can go. Her eyes saw a world now unimaginable to us. She was ten years old at the time of Victor Hugo's funeral, twenty at the time of the Dreyfus affair; she was a middle-aged woman when the soldiers of 1914 enthusiastically went off to battle. She could have known, as they say, Maupassant,

Verlaine, Zola, and Proust, Colette, Ravel, Modigliani, younger than her, long dead. You could use the outline of this small woman without history — all the more easily as she had no history — to mark all the pages of the century that she experienced. Unscathed, almost without memories, for the person people tended to credit with the century's collective memory could only remember the assassination of the Tsar's family in 1917. She was pure, biological time, freed of horror and upheaval.

August 12

In 95, during the heat wave in the United States, in Chicago, several hundred people died in poor areas, recluses in their homes, often from fear of going out. A hundred and eleven victims were unidentifiable, their bodies unclaimed by close relatives or friends. A mass funeral was organized. "Dug out and filled in by a bulldozer, the common grave measures more than one hundred and sixty yards. It has neither tombstone nor epitaph." (*Le Monde diplomatique*)

September 1

Diana died with her lover in a car accident, at the Pont de l'Alma, in the night between Saturday and Sunday.

Contrast between the great collective emotion aroused by Diana's death and the indifference toward that of dozens of people whose throats were slit in Algeria. We know nothing of the assassinated Algerians, of their lives; we knew everything about Diana, her marital woes, her children, her miniskirts. We had been following her story for years, a story with which a great many women identified: a princess but just like us. The story of the anonymous Algerians begins with their death. Neither their number nor the injustice and barbarity involved arouse any emotion. That is reserved for the individual story, for the face of a young, rich woman.

Diana's death requires nothing from us except tears for the injustice of destiny. It consoles. The death of people whose throats were slit in Algeria makes us ashamed of doing nothing.

October 24

In the bookstore at the Vancouver Airport, among the stacks of best-sellers on display, a book on orgasms, published by Smithbooks. On the publicity strip: "*The ultimate pleasure point: the cul-de-sac.*"

November 7

There'll be no more francs in three or four years. Instead, the euro. Unease, almost sorrow, in the face of this disappearance. From childhood to now, my life has been in francs, the Carambar candy — five old francs; the meal ticket for the university cafeteria — two francs, in the sixties; my illegal abortion — four hundred francs; my first salary — one thousand and eighty francs. In less than ten years, saying "I earned eight thousand francs" will be enough to place us in an era that has disappeared, making us anachronistic like the nobility of the nineteenth century who still counted in écus.

1997

November 11

Absolute silence where I am right now, in my house, a point in the indeterminate space of the new town. Experiment: via memory travel through the territory surrounding me, and in doing so describe and define the expanse of real and imagined space that is mine in the city. I go down as far as l'Oise — here is Gérard Philipe's house — cross over, survey the outdoor recreational area at Neuville, return via Port-Cergy, dash off toward l'Essec, the areas of Touleuses and Maradas, pass the Pont d'Éragny — I am in the Art de Vivre shopping center — return via Highway A15, turn off through the countryside to reach Saint-Ouen-l'Aumône, the Utopia Cinema, and Maubuisson Abbey. I pass over Pointoise in all directions, continue to Auvers-sur-Oise, go up the church hill, toward the cemetery, Van Gogh's grave covered in ivy. I return by the same road along the Oise, making a brief stop at Osny. I take the wide avenues leading to the center of Cergy-Préfecture: Trois-Fontaines, the Tour Bleue, the theater, the conservatory, and the library. I follow the RER line and the cavalcade of pylons to Cergy-Saint-Christophe, the big clock at the station. I walk along the street that leads me to the Tour Belvédère and the columns of the Esplanade de la Paix, from where an immense horizon unfolds, with, at the end, the shadows of la Défense and the Eiffel Tower.

For the first time, I have taken possession of space that I have been traveling through for twenty years.

November 30

They have gone back to their suburban city, east of Paris.

They arose at one in the afternoon. They had gone to bed that night at three o'clock after watching *X-Files* and playing computer games. They breakfasted around two o'clock and went to walk around Art de Vivre, the shopping center open on Sundays. They stayed for quite a while in the bookstore there, bought new games.

He had brought some laundry. I did two loads in the morning, in the afternoon ran the iron over his tee-shirts and jeans, his basic wardrobe.

Here I am noting the signs of the times, nothing personal: the Sunday of a single woman whose son comes to see her with his girlfriend, in the Paris area. Sorry I didn't attempt to grasp these details from the time I began writing, at age twenty-two: weekend of a girl of the sixties at her parents', in the country, etc., rather than wanting to record moods.

December 13

David Beaune, the skinhead who threw Imad Bouhoud, a young Beur, in the water at the docks of Le Havre, wrote in his diary: "It was April 18, St. Perfectus' Feast Day. It was cold. A craze for death swept through me.

"We went toward the Vauban basin [. . .], we threw 1997 him in the water. He sank. My thirst for blood was quenched [. . .]

"Remorse does not exist. I discovered, fascinated, that remorse was pure fiction."

This diary excerpt resembles a passage from a novel written in the first person. But it is not fiction; it is the exact transcription of feelings experienced after an actual murder, that of Imad Bouhoud. I was stunned by the last sentence, terrible and beautiful *in itself*. But Beaune would never have discovered that feeling, would never have written about it if he had not killed a boy his own age, simply because the boy was a Beur.

Is writing "acceptable" only if it is fiction? Doesn't writing, as in this case, aggravate the crime, justifying it by denying remorse? With this sentence by David Beaune, we must choose: either writing is outside morality, or it deals continually with morality.

1998

February 27

"Would you like a cup of coffee?" the hairdresser suggests. Then: "Would you like something to read?" Not a newspaper, a magazine, but an activity whose objective is indifferent, any printed matter in the magazine rack. Anyway, if you say yes, the hairdresser brings the newspaper closest at hand. But you could reason differently: understanding "something to read" in the same way as "some food," something "to read" as something "to eat."

March 25

In the early morning RER, a woman was putting on eye make-up, the mirror at nose level. Another was filing her nails, then polishing them. Carefully and slowly they performed these gestures among the crowd of travelers as if alone in their bathrooms. Superb freedom, or exhibition — hard to say. Their hands, their eyelids seemed to be distinct objects that they cleaned and lubricated in peaceful delight.

April 2

Papon has been condemned to ten years in prison. I don't know what to think. People said, "you have to put yourself back in time; things were not so clear then." That always means put yourself in the shoes of those who had nothing to fear, in their offices, in Vichy or elsewhere, never in those of the people who boarded trains for Auschwitz.

April 9

A guest on France Inter: the director of ADIE, the Association for the Right to Economic Initiative. What we hear immediately is the voice, not what it says. A voice that articulates each word, the way people do in Neuilly, a voice that does not speak, that pronounces. That does not know what it is to live on three thousand five hundred francs a month, let alone ten thousand.

For the first time today, at Auchan, I did not put the packaged bread that I no longer wanted back in the place where I'd taken it, too far away. I put it discreetly on the bags of cat litter. Ashamed of behaving this way, I imagine hundreds of products abandoned all over the place, deli meats left in the shoes, yogurt, desserts in the vegetable bins, etc. Customers no longer accepting the order imposed by the superstore — taking a basket or a cart, striding through the various sections, stretching out a hand toward the object, grabbing it, placing it in the cart or putting it back on the shelf, heading toward the cash, paying — but instead opening boxes of cookies, bottles of perfume, feeding themselves here and there according to their whim, wreaking chaos in every department and leaving without paying, of course. I asked myself why that never happened.

April 11

Memories in black and white of childhood, of all the years up to 1968. Memories in color afterwards. Hasn't memory followed the transition from movies and television from black and white to color?

April 12

Mazarine Pingeot is the classic example of the cultured, brilliant young woman who believes that these aptitudes lead naturally to writing a book. So she writes. She calls her novel *Premier roman — First Novel*. With this title, she is emphasizing her performance: *this is my first novel*, not much concerned about pulling in the reader by a word, a sentence creating desire or expectation. Titles, which also serve to distinguish books from one another, are good for humble folks, not for Mazarine Pingeot. However, she does not have enough of a belief in the value of her novel to risk handing it to a publisher without mentioning she is François Mitterrand's daughter. *First Novel* is reminiscent of "first dance." Forty years ago, middle class girls awaited this event to make their entry into society. Now they wait to make their entry with their first literary work: this is an improvement.

April 13

The RER stations were deserted on this Easter Monday morning. At Neuville-Université, on the platform heading to Paris, only one couple was hugging in silence, not moving. From the car heading toward Cergy, only the girl's back was visible. He had his head buried in her neck. When the RER started up again, her face was visible, a girl with glasses. She was looking straight ahead, into the distance. The train that one of them had to take was going to arrive, like the end of the world.

May 28

Getting off the RER at four in the afternoon at Fontenay-aux-Roses means arriving at a small country station. A few passengers quickly disband on the footbridge, heading toward rich-looking houses. No one selling fruit at the exit, no gatherings of people. No foreigners. At the station and in the surrounding area, all is calm, distant, limited to transportation. Here, there is no need for a station: it is just a stopping off point.

Cergy-Préfecture station, at the same hour, every day: constant motion, groups of young people, people selling strawberries and pizzas. Smells of the underground station, buses. Life.

June 2, 2008

Peculiar silence in the RER cars, which are nevertheless full, in early morning, around seven o'clock. As if people had brought along with them their unfinished night. In the evening, the reverse: vibrations everywhere, a purposeless energy that invisibly buzzes in the air. At the stop, people rush out. Seen from the lower level of the subway cars, legs running by, parallel with the window.

June 9

In the tenth arrondissement, the City of Paris social welfare agency is located in the basement of city hall. As soon as the metal gates open, people rush forward, go down the staircase, take a ticket, sit down. At the reception area, an employee is shouting at everyone. A man hands him his papers. "This is in Chinese! I don't understand Chinese," he cries. He moves towards the aligned chairs where people are waiting. "Does anyone speak Chinese?" No one answers. The employee returns to the man: "Nobody here speaks Chinese. Come back with an interpreter who speaks Chinese." The man remains motionless. The employee pushes him toward the door. A voice arises from the chairs: "Wait, perhaps he speaks English? Do you speak English?" The employee turns in the direction of the voice, roaring: "mind your own business!" The Chinese man leaves.

In the same room, parallel to the wall, a series of adjoining plastic bubble enclosures. In each one, a woman sitting behind a desk and two chairs in front. When the number is called, you appear at the entrance to the bubble; the woman says to sit down, asks why you are there, then for the papers. It is the confessional of the poor.

When you leave, the employee carefully cuts the dark part of a photocopy that he is responsible for handing over, while watching out for new arrivals, ready to make them feel his power and their unworthiness.

It is a place where only the destitute come, where the very hypothesis of the presence of other people is not imagined.

July 10

At the Gennevilliers Bridge, on Highway A15, all of a sudden, an immense opening onto Paris. Because of the traffic, people are never able to stop; they see the buildings, houses, the Eiffel tower slide by, right up to the moment when they disappear, to the right, toward la Défense, in the mass of stone that appeared a few seconds beforehand, moving, in an arc before the windshield.

1998

For twenty years the roads have been constantly changing here in the Colombes-Nanterre area that must be crossed to reach the Pont de Neuilly. From one year to the next the route is never the same. Vague memory of multiple itineraries, one that weaved around the buildings of la Défense, taking us onto suspended bridges, another that had us stopped for long minutes beneath a black bridge, close to the Université of Nanterre, another still, slaloming between building sites, before the mouth of the tunnel. Now we take a road that loops around to join Highway A15 at the exit of the tunnel. Everything happens as if the territory between la Défense and Colombes were unsettled, with roads being shifted continually, entangled above, below, in a gigantic aerial eight that can be dismantled and put back together a little further on. We wonder if, on this ground that has been moved, turned over, there are still people.

July 12

At the Trois-Fontaines boulangerie-pâtisserie, the salesclerk arrives from the kitchen with a rack of cakes. Only her right hand is gloved in rubber. She puts down the rack and begins to arrange the cakes in the window with the gloved hand and the other which is not. I wondered if that was the one she put up her ass.

(I could have simply told myself that it wasn't clean. Another way of thinking reality.)

July 19

This afternoon I went to the Jardin des Plantes. There were flowerbeds, roses, yet an imperceptible feeling of abandonment. I wanted to see the zoo again. The large tortoises were there, in their enclosure, but far away. Two yaks, one an adult, the other three months old, were slumped down along the wire fence. A stag was eating food spread out over the concrete. In the aviary, countless birds were crisscrossing, making a terrifying noise above stagnant water.

Further on, there were eagles and vultures beneath black foliage. One of them, wings spread, red head, crested, was acting like an exhibitionist. On the ground, dead rats were torn open. Sparrows and starlings kept flying in and out of the cage of the parrots, who were silent, transfixed on branches — circling around them, cheeping and pecking away at their seeds. Elsewhere, it was mice that were making the racket in the invisible animal's cage that leaned against a mound of earth from which the mice appeared suddenly, springing up.

Pictures by Chagall had been placed in the lion's cage. An enormous piano sat imposingly in the middle of the space reserved for the ostriches. Toward the back of the garden, strange little animals appeared, half rabbits, half dogs. On the sign, it said "maras." A llama was pissing and shitting; another was watching him. When the first one moved away, the second came to piss and shit at the same spot where already a pile of damp excrement was accumulating. It was very hot and the smell was very strong everywhere.

This is the most desolate spot in Paris you can get into for thirty francs.

August 4

In deserted Auchan, this morning, a pure sensation of happiness. I travel in the midst of abundance, between the various departments and stalls. Not looking at my shopping list, not worrying about time, gathering a bit of food here and there, like in a garden.

August 10

What R. likes in writing is the writer's life: the freedom, the feeling of belonging to a separate, superior population. Even the persistent effort of forcing out one page a day, this suffering that others cannot know, draws on the excellence of this life. The work itself, its capacity to act on people, is much less important.

August 16

Montparnasse Cemetery, divided up with military precision, with no shade. To the left of the entrance is Marguerite Duras' tombstone, strewn with bits of letters, a photo of her at age sixteen. The heat is overwhelming. Impossible to find Maupassant and Baudelaire among the gray tombs made identical by the weather. Only those of the last thirty years, in marble, can be spotted. Here is Serge Gainsbourg, properly buried with his parents. Next to him, a tombstone on which is written only one name, Claude Simon. A Japanese tourist photographs it. Perhaps she is unaware that the writer Claude Simon is not dead. Or does she want a fun photo to take home.

The visitors wander among the graves. People do not know what they have come looking for. All they find are names on stones. To the right of the entrance, Sartre and Beauvoir, together. She won for eternity. Little papers in all languages on their tombstone, a yellowish monument, too bright.

September 2

Three girls, ages six, four, and two, living in a transit camp near Grenoble, got into an abandoned car. The doors shut on them. The children were not able to get out and remained there for hours. When they were found, the youngest one was dead, the four-year old was in a coma. This resembles the beginning of the novel by Toni Morrison that came out in the spring, *Paradise*. Here, since this is reality, no one wants to talk about it.

September 14

Le Monde has published the partial translation of prosecutor Kenneth Starr's report on Bill Clinton's relationship with Monica Lewinsky. Perhaps because of cuts, the text resembles a poorly written, repetitive pornographic story: "He touched her breasts, unzipped his fly, etc." People end up forgetting that the character in the text is the President of the United States. It is the quite ordinary story of an ordinary, careful man, who does not really fuck, for fear of AIDs or of being surprised. Written sex makes the person seem average but maintains a kind of magic, which disappears with the last line.

The image of Clinton the other day was more obscene, when he said on television, "I have sinned. And I ask forgiveness, etc."

Monica Lewinsky belonged to an anti-abortion league. She knows everything about fellatio, but what does she know about abortion, of that experience, of its depths?

October 20

Today high school students demonstrated. Only the nice ones. To prevent the bad ones, the rioters, from joining them, police were deployed in the subway and the RER suburban stations. Quarantine line between the distant hordes of barbarians and the serious, clean young people in the center of Paris. In Cergy-Préfecture station, there was a riot policeman at every gate. A plain-clothes cop — shiny green suit — was watching people enter. A few Beurs were standing off in the distance. Today, only white people could take the train for Paris.

October 28

They are three young people, students no doubt, reading in the RER, one Foucault's *History of Sexuality*, the others, philosophical works. A woman entered and sat down with her child in the same row as them, on the other side of the aisle. The child plays with a toy, a mobile phone that makes cat noises, ringing, a woman's voice, and other sounds emerge from it as well. The students begin ostentatiously to show their annoyance; they lean forward abruptly and look insistently at the child's toy. The mother, a black woman, pays them no attention — or cannot decipher their gestures. The child is three or four, difficult to keep quiet. The students seem increasingly infuriated. Everything they have read or learned about cultural differences and tolerance does not help them at this precise moment. Perhaps even philosophy upholds their right to not be disturbed in their reading, in the name of the superiority of the world of ideas over the real world.

November 4

The Administrative Court of Paris. Nine foreigners
without papers appear, alone or with their lawyer, to
ask that their APRF, the expulsion order, be revoked.
The place is beautiful, with velvet banquettes in the
foyer. A young lawyer arrives, robe over her arm, slips
it on. Then another one arrives. People enter the room,
large and dark, almost empty. The presiding judge is
not there. A three quarter of an hour wait. The prefect's
representative, in her fifties, is seated, face inscrutable,
files spread out in front of her. An African family, father,
mother, five children, have sat down before the court.

The presiding judge arrives. He is alone at the back,
far away. His face appears blurred. The room is dimly
lit. It is difficult to hear him. The young lawyer pleads
for three minutes for the man with the five children.
The woman he is living with has her papers in order; he
is raising the four children she had with another man,
and a fifth born of their union. The prefect's representative gets up heavily, basically says that this man has no
reason to remain in France.

Fatimata N's lawyer now has her turn. She rapidly
goes over the arguments of the brief she drafted to
appeal the expulsion order, then asks the presiding
judge if I may say a few words on behalf of Fatimata
N. The judge answers "yes, if it doesn't take too long."
I approach the bar. I try to formulate rapidly the reasons why Élisabeth Fatimata N. should have the right
to remain legally in France. In the distance, the presid-

ing judge stares at me impassively. I have the impression I'm giving a bad performance, having no effect on anyone. The prefect's representative rises, presents her arguments against waiving the expulsion order. It is over, ten minutes in all.

That evening I learn that all this morning's appeals have been rejected.

November 21

Today the weather is clear and freezing cold; the media announce that a woman has died of cold in Toulouse and three homeless people in Paris. Saying "homeless people" is to designate a sexless species who carry bags and wear worn-out clothing, whose steps go nowhere, without past or future. It is saying that they are no longer normal people.

In France there are thirty million dogs and cats that people would never think of leaving outside in such weather. We let men and women die in the street, perhaps precisely because they are our fellow men, with the same desires and needs as us. It is too difficult to put up with this part of ourselves, dirty, stupefied by the lack of everything. The Germans living near the concentration camps did not believe that the Jews in flea-ridden rags were people.

During the coldest night, a couple of unemployed workers, about fifty years old, took refuge in the toilet of a cemetery, with a puppy.

December

On the radio, *Les corons*, a song about mining villages by
Pierre Bachelet that was heard frequently in 81, the year
the left came to power. It evokes coal, silicosis, unending
poverty, and Jean Jaurès, in a kind of terrible rumbling:
a century of oppressed masses. It was a song in harmony
with the hopes of the times, with the imagination of the
Popular Front, with the red rose. And during that time
reality moved inexorably forward: unemployment and
lay-offs, stock-market speculation, poverty.

Sitting on the concrete in the subway station; head
hanging down and hand held out. Hearing footsteps,
seeing legs go by, the ones that slow down, hoping.
What would I prefer, that or prostituting myself, public
or private shame. Need to confront the extreme forms
of dereliction, as if there were a truth that could only
be discovered by paying this price.

1999

Fifty cars set on fire in Strasbourg, sixteen in Rouen, eight in Le Havre, and others as well in Bordeaux, Toulouse, by "suburban youths," according to the expression that differentiates those youths from others. They celebrated the New Year by burning society's cult object. Which, incidentally, the same day killed fifty people, without unduly upsetting anyone.

In Strasbourg, the city had planned New Year's festivities for "them," thus hoping to keep them calm. This was taking them for half-wits incapable of understanding the maneuver or for wild animals to be tamed. They brutally demonstrated that they were free to choose their celebration.

January 2

Sales. All entrances to the Trois-Fontaines parking lot are blocked by lines of cars. People want to be the first to throw themselves at the clothes, dishes, like plunderers in a conquered city. The aisles are inundated by a flood of people, entire families with children in strollers, groups of girls. In the stores, frenzy. A tremendous lust to acquire fills the air.

The shopping center has become the most familiar place in this end of century, like the church in times past. Chez Caroll, Froggy, Lacoste: people are seeking something to help them live, relief from time and death.

January 5

Dental surgery department at Pontoise Hospital. Three people are waiting at the admitting counter, each holding his or her file. The secretary, loud and clear, is on the phone to someone who apparently used to work in the department, gives them news of so and so, calls a nurse to hand her the receiver, takes it back then, "I have to stop. I have people!"

All doors are open. The double doors that connect the waiting room with the large corridor of the area reserved for surgery. The doors of the offices set out on each side of the long corridor. Extreme agitation is in the air; nurses circulate from one office to the other, call out to each other, joke: "I'm free now! (meaning that no doctor is calling for them). "Oh! Okay, I thought you were married!" Laughter.

They had me sit in an armchair. One of the two young women laying out the instruments for my operation asks the other if her shoes are comfortable. "Oh yes! And you know, I have knee problems." "A ligament?" "No, skiing, a long time ago now." "I should buy the same ones. Where did you get them?" There are women who are interested in shoes when, in two minutes' time, the surgeon will appear in the office and sever a piece of my gums.

January 8

The media have had a lot to say about the "children from the projects" who went to do winter sports in a "calm" sports resort (which seems rather an anomaly), and who disturbed the stay of the usual vacationers. People quoted a little five-year-old girl who called the ski instructor a slut and a bitch. As if that provided some kind of decisive proof: savageness, irrevocable impossibility of being like other children. In the mouth of the little girl, however, "slut and bitch" mean nothing more than "mean and nasty" in the language of children from nice neighborhoods. It reveals *no difference in nature* (contrary to what people try to imply).

January 11

In the evening, the trip back by RER is broken up into two phases. Up until Maisons-Lafitte, sometimes even up until Achères, takes the same amount of time as the trip out: no waiting. The traveling time, accepted, imperceptible, where people can think more or less. In the ten final minutes before arriving at the destination, there is another phase in which nothing exists except the need to get there. The regular movements of the train, the increasingly less built-up landscape, the stretch of fields, from the perspective of the inner clock everything seems slowed down. Impossible to think of anything during this time period. Longing only for the moment to leave the train, climb up the steps toward the exit, go through the turnstile, the cool air of the parking lot, the car. Hardly clear images, just an instinctive thrust toward what is a form of happiness. Each evening the same empty ten minutes: pure waiting.

January 12

On TV there is a report on a home for young delinquents in Marcq-en-Baroeul, in the North. All boys, supervised only until five o'clock and then free all evening. They don't know what to do, smoke pot in the rooms, "one joint and things are better right away." They never speak of school, as if it had never existed in their lives. Some don't know how to read. Many don't know that you begin writing at the top of a page in a notebook; they start in the middle, at the bottom, anywhere. They say that nothing matters except having fun (damaging cars, etc.) and not getting caught. They are sure that later, they will feel they made the most of being young ("if being young is working on your homework, without messing around, that's not a life"). Messing around is a synonym for pleasure. It is not goods they want most, but pleasure: defiance, dope, etc. And that is what we cannot see, what is more terrifying than the books by the Marquis de Sade because it is raw, without conceptualization or aesthetic distance.

January 15

On the platform at Cergy station, on the bottom of the sign indicating the stations it says *Pont Cardinet*. Neither the train nor the RER stop there.

February 15

D. is talking about the stores of Cergy, broaches the topic of "quality" clothing. He is wearing a Marks & Spencer sweater, Weston's, which he points out. "I give my Lacostes to my daughter," he says. Reciting the brands that he wears like claims to fame. He doesn't know that in a more fashionable world, people no longer wear Lacoste since the "suburban youths" have taken a shine to it. To tell him would no doubt hurt him deeply. Brands are symbols meant to indicate where we see ourselves in terms of social standing.

(Memory of S., putting his clothes back on one evening, proudly listing, in his Slavic accent, each garment
he put on, "a Cerrito shirt, a Dior tie, Saint Laurent
pants, a Levin belt, etc." Like the pieces of armor of a
knight in the Middle Ages donned religiously. Underneath, he wore a white undershirt and a shapeless pair
of briefs from an East Bloc country.)

March 24

The reporter gives the results of a survey: "There are too
many Arabs," is the response of 42 percent of French
people questioned. Adding, "racist views are becoming commonplace." The sentence "there are too many
Arabs" is the only one people really retain. If they sub-
stituted "Jews" in place of Arabs, they would notice that
there is no great difference between 1999 and 1939. This
survey and the way of presenting it insidiously justify
racism. In the imagination, what is only an opinion
becomes truth.

March 26

This train from Paris to Montargis stops at every station. This one is called Bourbon-Marlette. On the entire
surface of a blind wall, faded paint where it says, in huge
letters, *Dubonnet*.

Further on, another stop at a station whose name is
not visible from the compartment window. Along the
platform, a wall with small vertical cement bars, joined

by a horizontal one, evenly indented — so gray now that it looks like an old and fragile structure. A wall that used to run along the platforms of all stations in France and that children climbed while waiting for the train to arrive.

No one got on or off.

March 27

NATO has decided to "intervene" with the Serbs. Impression, as usual, of not knowing what is right. I see Belgrade in the evening, the main square and the cafés teeming with people, gypsy children running from one table to another whom no one pushed away (paternalism, certainty of being superior, or kindness?) Belgrade at dawn, the stream of buses boarded by people against whom war is waged today. But I have no images or memories of the Kosovars.

April 6

Every night bombs rain down on Belgrade and the cities of Serbia. At the same time, Serbian soldiers calmly continue their acts of violence in Kosovo, forcing the Kosovars to flee. Strange choreography of death, vertical and horizontal, on separate stages. We can imagine that NATO bombs will rain down endlessly on the Serbian population and the Serbian soldiers pushing long lines of Kosovar's along the roads of exile. There is no mathematical chance of the missiles and the Serbian criminals meeting up.

Yesterday, Easter Monday: people were eating on terraces, along the seashore, in Normandy. Hours of traffic jams on the highway, in the evening, toward Paris. I noticed that for an entire afternoon I hadn't thought even once about the war in the Balkans. What is the value, the usefulness of such *thoughts*?

April 10

The war in the Balkans continues without giving rise to much reaction or reflection, as opposed to the war in the Gulf eight years ago. From now on destruction and death appear to be a necessary evil. We are also making the Serbian population pay for our lack of intervention in Bosnia. It is a war of catching up.

Experiencing this horrible feeling of weariness at hearing and reading the same things: "strikes" by NATO on Serbia, Kosovar refugees flocking into cities whose names were unknown three weeks ago and that now seem as familiar as Saint-Nazaire and Chambéry: Blace, Podgorina. Familiarity that destroys the interest in what, in any case, remains a show.

April 13

Sunday, on TV, a guy from NATO is talking about military operations in the Balkans. Good-looking, very elegant, jacket and tie that match beautifully. His superb tie is the discouraging detail, the insolent sign that the person speaking about war will never be among those who wage it.

1999

Feeling of becoming accustomed to the vision of all the suffering of this war. And perhaps more to the sight of human suffering than to the destruction of bridges, trains, etc.

This evening, on TV France 2, intellectuals and politicians are debating the war. At the same time, TF1 is showing two cheerful guys asking a girl with a magnificent, smooth face, her measurements. "34–25–31," she replies in one breath. The guys ask her for specifics. She needs no persuading: "34 bust, 25 waist, 31 hips." She is a supermodel, describes what she experiences on stage, walking down the runway. One day, she looked down at the people seated in the orchestra and saw Jean-Paul Gaultier smiling at her. It was . . . She is at a loss for words. Finishing up, one of the two overexcited hosts warns us: "Remember this name well: *Julie*! You'll be hearing about her!" Applause. Admittedly this world where beauty and success are values, where Jean-Paul Gaultier has the smile of God, still exists.

April 14

In the falling snow, a man was asking for food at the lights of a major crossroads on the National Highway.

Twentieth day of war. Packages pour in for the Kosovar deportees and thousands of people offer to take a family into their homes. The exodus of the Kosovars strikes the imagination: brutal, collective, attributable to one sole cause, Milošović. It is a misfortune where the victims have no share in the responsibility, nor any recourse. An absolute tragedy. (Anouilh said that in such a case, people are calm). And the women wear headscarves and long skirts like our peasants used to do.

Illegal immigrants and homeless people, the unemployed, arouse only indifference. This is slow misfortune, isolated, that exists for many reasons, that does not draw attention to itself. We doubt that the victims have no responsibility in that (*after all*, there are shelters where people can sleep, work to be had if they make an effort to look for it, etc.). This particular misfortune calls for something other than packages.

June 18

The war in the Balkans has ended. The violent debates on television on the legitimacy of the bombings, the images of exodus and destruction seem to belong to a faraway past. For us this war was absolutely nothing.

On the wall of the train station parking lot, now, in huge letters: *Lehla I love you*.

August 11

Around twelve ten, the light began to fade. Large shadows fell over the grass in the garden. It was the light of dreams and of the past. Silence won out. There was a racket in the branches of the fir tree across from the terrace; a squirrel had fallen from the top like a stone. Immediately afterward there followed a clear night, coolness. The lamps from the street below were lit. It seemed to me to go on for a very long time. I was not sure of seeing what I was seeing because I had never seen that before. The light returned only very slowly.

I continued to look at the black disc slipping in front of the sun, shrinking. At one forty, the Moon had stopped passing in front of the Sun. Feeling of desolation, the same that, in my childhood, came when things were over, a movie, a day at the seashore. A void, sucking me up toward the outside.

With everyone, in these last months of the century, a strange feeling of history. The play will end, and we discover all of a sudden that we are the actors. *We will pass over the Earth* . . .

August 14

The broadcast of the show *L'enfant et les sortilèges* by Ravel and Colette was delayed; on the third channel the news was still on. The newscaster was saying that "since 91, the Gulf War — we have perhaps forgotten — *a half million* Iraqi children have died, due to lack of care and food." He continued immediately, with the enthusiastic tone of an auctioneer, "but, the U.S. announces that it will give *a million* dollars to restore Iraqi hospitals." Which puts the Iraqi child at two dollars, ten or twelve francs, depending on the exchange rate. Then he showed images of children at the hospital, emaciated and prostrate in tiny beds with bars. Later, he quoted the UN Security Council stating that in the area where the distribution of supplies and medication was entrusted to this organization, "only *twenty percent* of children were dying." The newscaster seemed happy to be able to provide us with so many figures.

Afterwards, finding the meowing of cats, the sad cries of shepherd boys, the dance of the Indian teapot and the English teacup, all the charm and foolishness of *L'enfant et les sortilèges* dated, frivolous. The delicate dream of an opulent, western middle class whose chubby-cheeked, big-bottomed Child, played by a soprano, seemed to be the grotesque descendant.

Things seen in the outside world require everything; most works of art, nothing.

September 1

They appear suddenly from the northwest, from behind the trees and buildings upon the hills of Cergy. They cross the immense sky of the loop around l'Oise, toward Roissy, tirelessly tearing apart the September light.

Invincible noise pollution of air traffic: at the beginning of each rumbling, waiting for the sound track to pass through the head and move on, waiting for the next one, living with the rhythm and hum of the airplanes.

One day, the entire sky will become "aerial," criss-
crossed with routes that are noisier than those on the ground, invaded by aircraft that will collide with one another and fall, causing ten thousand deaths a year, above and below. In cruel indifference, as is now the case with car accidents. This is how men resemble gods.

October 28

The Russians are calmly exterminating the Chechens. No one gets upset. Are there really people with names that seem to come right out of a tale by Voltaire? People have gotten into the habit of seeing the history of Russia as a bloody fiction, with frozen steppes, vodka, mon- sters, and mummies or buffoons for main characters. That Yeltsin is all three at once is only the saga taken to perfection and the chapter of the Chechens is in the same vein as the preceding ones. Russia's impunity stems obscurely from its myth about people at the furthermost bounds of space, reason, humanity.

November 4

Visible on a wall at Cergy station: the half-folded legs of a man in blue corduroys, between which are squeezed those of a woman wearing a dress with small white and green checks. The woman is seen from the front, the last buttons of her dress are open on her bare legs. It is a hippy fresco, dating from the late seventies, which will soon be erased when the station is renovated.

Someone has thrown red paint at the dress, at the place where the vagina would be, it forms a bloody spatter.